maMa DaDa

maMa daDa

SONGS OF THE BARONESS'S DOG

BY JaN JHorneR

TURNSTONE PRESS

Mama Dada: Songs of the Baroness's Dog
copyright © Jan Horner 2009

Turnstone Press
Artspace Building
018-100 Arthur Street
Winnipeg, MB
R3B 1H3 Canada
www.TurnstonePress.com

Turnstone Press gratefully acknowledges the assistance of the Canada
Council for the Arts, the Manitoba Arts Council, the Government of
Canada through the Book Publishing Industry Development Program,
and the Government of Manitoba through the Department of Culture,
Heritage, Tourism and Sport, Arts Branch, for our publishing activities.

Cover design: Jamis Paulson
Interior design: Sharon Caseburg
Cover photograph: Claude McRay [sic] and Baroness Von
Freytag-Loringhoven, c. 1927 (Library of Congress, Bain Collection).
Printed and bound in Canada by Friesens for Turnstone Press.

Library and Archives Canada Cataloguing in Publication

Horner, Jan C. (Jan Cynthia), 1952–
    Mama dada : songs of the baroness's dog / Jan Horner.

Poems.
ISBN 978-0-88801-344-6

    1. Freytag-Loringhoven, Elsa von, 1874-1927--Poetry.
I. Title.

PS8565.O6696 M36 2009   C811'.54   C2009-900716-9

for David

CONTENTS

mᵃMₐ Dₐᵈ𝒶

The Baroness meets her Mars

I am entitled to be deeply shocked.
                              — the Baroness

Snappy with electrical charges
an instrument strung and vibrating
my own little seaside resort with its
octopus love pillow, sweet and salty,
ruby-throated. *Remove your helmet, mister.*
Press the buzzer, I'll take you in.
My rose smiling, its succulent petals
muscled and tender. *Unsheath your light*
sword, superman, swing me radiant
across the night sky, catch me falling
the energy crackling, flaring in bursts
your Frankenstein to my mrs
our own super charged light show.
A serenade rising and falling, our
midnight groans, until
torched with thunderbolts, ripped
open, both hooked and gasping,
lightning having licked us negative…

don't you hear it Mars? the waves
lapping, cool and salty over cockles
shell land, the sea dogs hushed, panting.

SONGS OF THE BARONESS'S DOG

Advice to a corseted poet

afflicted people should stay home—
with family—friends.

— the Baroness

See if it can make you happy
this life in two rooms
with one egg in the fridge
and seven pairs of scissors.

You're standing in the doorway
with restless hands and tapping feet
waiting, hearing only voices
from those places you can't trust
the diaphragm and pelvic cave.
You're riddled with conceits
your head lousy with language
useless with fitful energies
pressing PANIC
punky with escapes.

Live outside your placid comfort
the familiar level crossings,
undam the passive, remote controls
cut open those gelid veins.
Squat on the roof
of your most immodest desires
step out and strut among
your fellow *saltimbanques*
the likewise daring and unconstrained.

Concede nothing, whatever happens
roll them over on their backs
leave them defenseless, those hapless readers.
Murder your doubt
just reign.

Maybe

vielleicht

your mother had
syphilis, a present
from your pop.
Something curdled
inside her brain
and led her away.
They found her
days later, content and safe
in a neighbour's attic
playing a doll's house
game.

kann sein

you escaped to Berlin
into theatre and that time
of *every night another man*
who fed you, gave you a bed.
You were forced
to follow a treatment,
a public hospital to your horror.
Maybe the doctors were right
your syphilis was congenital.

You were one of the few
not stillborn, or miscarried,
umarked by
thin hair, soft bones
baby teeth.

es mag sein

you were never pregnant
although so promiscuous
you weren't as wild
as you suggest,
maybe you knew
a good abortionist
or was he a butcher?
And what did Djuna know
who said in *Nightwood*
of her heroine Robin,
your alter-ego: she had

>   *the iris of a beast*
>   *not tamed to meet*
>   *the human eye.*

die Möglichkeiten

Greve never forgave you
left with no conscience
and while you camped with
negroes in Kentucky
he went north to the raw frontier
married a Mennonite schoolmarm
his sister-wife, and mourned
not for you or himself
your youthful promise long
tarnished and forsaken,
but saved his forlorn
sorrow for the early death of
his only daughter.

perhaps

you were never satisfied
not even with Marcel Marcel,
whom you loved like hell,
your disease and Nike energy
lack of domestic science,
the stigma, and true secret of
your failure with American men.

Maybe you were damaged by Adolph-papa,
the wrong hidden by the driver Fernand?
One more reason beyond the sniffing
stepmama to run away
and you went on coupling
despite knowing you were
a *shame-mangled monster*
and you kept on
looking for trouble
always wanting the lead.

Consider me a fish… that is left on [a] bone-dry beach by crazy time's tide! Put me into [the] sea again! I will swim…

— the Baroness

it may be

your cure was spontaneous,
the infection lay dormant,
or could the dragon have started
its undoing and you alone knew it,
the suicide of your grandfather
      a gaping solution and you took
yourself by the tail and threw your body
into the sea with no ceremony,
but with a fear of being alone
reached out for Pinky-dog
to drown with you
in the gassy waves.

As if

you could
know
by her skirt
tossing
morning
in her stride
and she could
ignite
with her red
petticoat
the town
in Titian
flame.

as if
she could
stop
his lips
kissing
the hem
of her red slicker
his fire-fears
heart
pomegranate
scarlet
pubicities.

as if
she was a
red-blooded
baroness
a genuine
heroine
shimmering
ruby-veined
cinnamon-scented
rose
carmine.

as if
she could fly
ruby-slippered
her feet
shiny
valentines
the first wave
from a red
planet
repelling meteors
with her
feet.

as if
insurance
could prevent
accidents
your brains
the baboon's
rosy hind parts
dashed
on the street
as if
she could
throw on
the crimson
ball gown
dodging
brimstone,
set madder sails
and soar
from the roof.

In which

I tell the Baroness in words coming furious and breathless, my car has been vandalized and she tells me she has lost and found everything except her virginity and her teeth, how she never owned an automobile but had been mugged and they took her woolworthless jewellery, a violation nonetheless. How she lifted things herself only when she was needy, an umbrella, a bright piece of nothing, and she couldn't understand the outrage of her pursuers, calling her klepto-thief, when the only sin is hoarding and marking something for yourself that belongs to everyone, like air or water, a beautiful view, or those precious books that stand eager and unread on library shelves.

Else's beautiful game

Else thinks they're amateurs, the fans
with painted faces, partisan hats
the team colours, scarves, and shirts.
She could teach them a thing or two
about the costume game, about warrior
rattle and atavistic mask.

But what are they watching
with their deafening roars
and drunken songs: an ebb and flow
of colourful bodies and leviathan cheers:
A ball played from chest to foot, foot to chest
through legs, the artful flicking passes
skirted shorts meeting deft tackles
whipping heads and bicycle kicks.
And yes the rippling thighs and calves
the sweaty purity of toughened chests
and bellies, no time for
anything but the body's thoughts
split second reflex, diving save
immaculate balance and the solemn wall:
five men meekly shield their balls
protecting virility and their goal.

Else points to the boards around the pitch
don't you see how they argue
amongst themselves:
AMSTEL beer licks CARLING clean
PLAYSTATION outscores MASTERCARD
ADIDAS puts the boot to Queen NIKE's balls!
Inspired, she begins to call the plays:

Lonely Guy passes to *Rough and Ready*
who punts it onto *Little Big Man* waved onside
who loses it to *Arms and Legs*—no foul.
Bloody Minded tackles cleanly—no fool
and the ball goes out of play for a corner kick.
Spice Boy crosses the ball to *High Flyer*
to head down for *Dreadlocks* to balloon over the bar.
Now *Off His Game* boots it down the pitch
for *Lionheart* to flick onto the head of
Underachiever to nod home unmarked by
Brave Poodle, beyond the reach of *Very Lonely Guy*
and the crowd roars for the poetry and sheer relief.

Else decides she can't sit still, she must join
the action and command the field—wait
she replaces the ref, takes the whistle and little black book
exchanges words with foul play boys
runs about writing her own rules,
flashing cards, issuing cautions
a penalty or two, stopping short of showing red.
At full time she anoints a champion
based on skill and flair, ignoring goals
the erupting protest, abuse from the crowd.
The linesmen have had it, confiscate her whistle
and the hero *Brave Poodle* arrives, with a wink to me
a smile on his face and escorts the poets off the pitch.

The Baroness on parade, Christopher Street Day (Berlin) 2001

1
Yours with devotion, trumpet and drums
heavenly saltimbanques straight from heaven.
A thousand [hankies]
and as many bandwagons filled with showmen
tumblers, dancing, no thoughts of safety
from ribald parents, rascals
straight from heaven,
dance hellions

and damn
mrs hetero-
nor – mal

2
Truck upon truck of writhing bodies
bouncing to Abba or techno-pop.
Men undressed or dressed as women
fair queens, a dominatrix or two
a dusting housewife, giddy models of lingerie.
And women in t-shirts, sober, pouting
sensible, braless and promoting health,
outnumbered in a throng of biceps,
pecs, buttocks and only one penis
to Else's dismay, yet nothing could
stop her joining the fun in a tomato-can bra
flying helmet and her striped pantaloons.

Else, doesn't this somehow lack an edge—
a body is a boob is a bottom is a box—
where's the design, where's the art in that?

And where's the shock when the hetero-tourists
bring toddlers to watch
the rainbow children on a day out
acting up in raucous tribute?

But Else watches me rubberneck a kilted man
skin-head, t-shirt, sandals, socks
on a street pillar his perfect form
mechanically dances, a cross-gender general
greeting his troops and like Else I wonder
what's under the kilt, as another
flat truck of bare-chested boys comes past
and all but lost in the sea anemone
of waving arms, one girl, her long white
arm, bracelet and cigarette extending out from
a graceful torso and young round bare breasts
artfully freckled, she catches my gawk
giving back an angry stare, I sense
her power and responsive dare, and Else laughs
as if to taunt: what's under your skirt?
and what's this about art?

The late Baroness Else goes cycling

The late Baroness reads my mail, asks who's this Bob-boy
with his bike? He's the Bob travelling in central Europe,
the wonder bred boy, moving each year behind an
executive father, onward and upward. He's Bob, in love
with unmotorized movement—wooden canoes, sleek
bicycles—and going nowhere.

In disbelief I watch the Baroness squeeze into lime and
fuchsia shorts, making sure I admire her legs and boyish
hips. With the sense of a hound she tracks Bob down,
measuring his pace, then cruising in his wake. They're
both past fifty, high on movement, and still amazed at
the view. Both new to this central Europe aglide those
hills from Dresden along the Elbe in love with speed and
conversation. Else acquires his taste for beer—she wants
to sit astride his saddle, fly along a spoon to his back. But
he can't hear or feel her, is too attentive to the girlie-girls
in Poland. And then Bob flies off, head over heels—she's
manoeuvred his fall. But to everyone's surprise he's a
bionic man, back in the saddle, two days later off on the
trail.

Back to his dogs and his single life—she likes dogs, but
those snuffling terriers, those feisty hunters, after a life
of running, boxing, she wants something more sedate,
more Pekinese. O to be cradled, every whim or need
met, each sneeze admired, untroubled by spokes, libidos,
ghosts. She watches my friend ride away, knows Felix, all
black and throbbing on his Indian motorcycle, will zoom
up soon. Unfazed by her get-up, he'll shout: hey baby,
hop on!

Extraordinary food for extraordinary dogs

No dosing—Just rub it on.
                              — the Baroness

One world revolves around you
where do you want to go today?
what if there were a magic box
think where it would take you.
Drivers wanted.

Say yes it's all within your reach
the right technologies right now
could your heart use an extra twenty valves
the ultimate driving machine.
Some day all watches will be made like this.

I've searched Europe to find the secrets
of beautiful hair
old taste from the old place
and who will you be
in the next twenty-four hours? news that stays news
nothing tastes better from thought to finish
extraordinary food for extraordinary dogs.
Elegance is an attitude.

If a radio were turned on
this page would be in colour
this isn't scented
unless you smell the future
sometimes you need a little finesse
go ahead get dirty
reach out and touch someone
take what you want
because you're worth it

it's the real thing
        be   *extra*   direct
        ordinary
    dogs
                        just do it.

P-daddy speaks poet-to-poet

Put down that knife, madam
you are no surgeon
           drag your chair to the moonlight
           call up your muses, give Ez a buzz
remember
           the lost flower of Languedoc
           the middle kingdom
forget your sunshine's talks on
the deranged school of Austrian finance
or Monsieur Bouff – ay
           with money they try to buy beauty
           after it has died, with a grimace
           Beauty is ever dead—deada than dada
Absent thee from such felicity
           for Elsa Kassandra alias
           femme nikita
           the great trans – sister
           or was it great resister
           from the war on germs & filth
           conscientious objector

And the literati—Billy Carlos
djungle june, abel sanders
their ilk did not defend her
She deserved the bughouse no more than
   you or Ez with his grand idees

           she had not the sense
           to pace in harness
                foaming away her spirit
                       upon the bit

For all I know

For all I know
you are not listening
the dog knows as much
war wages on inside her
and it's down to me
the hem there to be lifted
where death sits waiting
its eartips lovesick
a leaping dog ready to nose it
for all I know we are skunked.

For all I know she was hateful
no innocent as she would have it
why keep a dog and bark yourself.
Always ready with insult, contumely
a witty poem with blackmail
in its core, for all I know
the cupboard was bare.

She could have exterminated rats
as she went to the dogs, but didn't
a bark worse than her bite, selling papers
on the Ku'damm, dog eat dog.
Nothing productive, no domestic breeder
a dogsbody, all in all ripe
to be gassed: indigent, aging
godless, diseased, a wretch
with dubious papers,
a worthless title, for all I know
her only passport: the junkyard art
the brave, unreadable poems.

I am your tango onto the page

Closing the book on the disconsolate day
my efforts doubt themselves and unwind
the shuffled cards peek from fifty-two angles
an earring tinkles, the toadking dreams
death wails disturb my ragged knitting
now dropped into this slow eddy
a listless cupboard of vacant thought.
UND KOMM JETZT MIT MIR!
She drags me out to rock and shake.
Listen, you be you, and still me be me
as I insist on stuffing everything in
with equal fury you pull most of it out.
While in me your world diminishes
complaints of too-soft couches, cushions,
honey, yours stinks of none too clean.
I want a shower and three new peignoirs
you need a smoke, a dada-boss shrink.

I am your tango onto this page
red-eyed sailor and androgyne, I let you lead
bending me over sex to sex
drowning reproach and tinfoil longings
we are tipsy, silenced, somnambular
starry finalities may beckon us on
but we move no further, held
          here on the edge of our uneasy truce.

Goldelse

Each day for four weeks the S-Bahn ride
from Zoo to Hackescher Markt and each day
Viktoria greeted me three times along the way
her gold resplendent in mid-morning light,
the last sight of her, far off, her forward tilt
from behind making her into a fairy
godmother above the trees. Her salute became
a sign, Viktoria Goldelse, insisting
I would succeed.

Viktoria—as if just alit from France,
Königsplatz, some neverland—
winged and eagled, freighted with stuff:
a staff, a wreath, a Grecian dirndl
[why not some little dog?]
a goddess above those mortal men—
Bismarck, the Counts Moltke and Roon—
with her flying skirts and metal cap
supported by sixty gilded cannons
trophies from Austria Denmark France.

No blood, no tears
distress her form so separate
from the fallen and crippled,
she floated down to them
after the drama had cooled
a bestower of laurels
on the dying and bloodied,
their mythic instant—a flash
before the sun went down.

After the Great War with its
bitter sorrows
and worse humiliations,
after the Kaiser quit,
leaving hollowed out myths
and tarnished symbols,
Viktoria lost her lustre.
With her chaste robe,
her wings too tinkerbell
for her girth and size,
was she ever the emblem
of a nation's fate,
its debut on
a modern stage?

Today directing traffic round Berlin's Great Star,
a lookout for sightseers who now and then
pause to peer up her skirts, and note
her gold leaf wearing thin,
a cold war shoulder for film stars
to look down from, a vantage point
from which they longed for mortal skins.
Like Else she embodies a bright new world,
touching down from her tarnished myth
while Else lifts up from her exiled past,
Goldelse and the Baroness, both likeable gals
with fancy names, they move towards us
on muscular feet, reclad, restored, re-storied
phoenixes freed from the rubble of time.

MAMA DADA

The Ride

We were hurtling along in the Benz
did we know where we were going
our whole family and Fernand the driver
my dad's pal in front, the blue uniform.
We were looking for mother
off her rocker again, heading through woods
down to the lake, the site of her last attempted
escape. No, she is here, sitting beside me
out of it, wrapped in her fine foulard.

Papa's blood is up, flushed with beer
his gun loaded for bear, cocked for the kill
looking for targets, looking for game.
I am the small girl, wanting his weapons
the power to make everyone shut up and listen
his physique and stamina, part of the thrill
of watching him perform. I want to be
his son, carrying his bag, I want his blue
twinkle eyes and laugh.

My mother, now no more out of it
than we are, warns me he'll eat me alive if I let him
just as he'd eaten her with his blood lust
he'd soiled her and he'd soil me and
we'd all burn in hell.

Remarried, he was always angry
as if I were a bad servant who returned his
laundry unclean and I felt tainted
with something I couldn't name
My life was split from that time forward
one part a fiction I made up

one part what the world made me
like her the thwarted artist
zany performer, like him the hunter
a seducer with his dragon heart.

Little Sister

Who shall say I am not/ the happy genius of my household?
— William Carlos Williams

You sniff at my clothes and hair
the way I move and look at men.
What energy you give to shame
from your ample seat, your domestic throne
content with your daughter-wife role
you wash your hands of me.

I've made bad choices, choosing
cold men, tight and ambitious, how much worse
to stay locked behind some door like you
hoarding your flesh, its priceless pearl.
My body is the performance—and perhaps
I will have nothing to show for it, but
what good will it do me dead.
And what of your pride in spic and span
little house frump from back of beyond
I was a baroness, I dressed dada
I loved dada, I lived dada.

And you little sister with your man
a pair of oxen in twin yokes
pulling the property of your merger
measuring out grains of affection
against degrees of comfort
go on, sustain your flesh house
what keeps you precious
lubricate the gears
of your household
and condemn mine—

you are entitled to your opinion
beautiful sister, and
fuck you.

Pretty things

1
tassled fan
demurring
chatter, bustle
a swag and
peacock flourish

light hands
tear translucent
tissues
palaver, soften
her correctives
corset
mummy-stiff

baffling
net, screen
protective blinds
hidden placket
couched fire
naked
without a hat

2
when he hits a sweet note
I call him *mr. pretty*

3
what you put up with for a good meal
a bed, a few pretty things:
silk patterned stockings
low-heeled Louis quinze slippers
embroidered bag and beaded sheath
parasols, feathers, kid gloves with
contrast stitching, lace
pink glowing earlobes
diamond starred.

4
not so pretty things:
bald heads
familiar forms of address
having to ask
impatient pressing
police court
the need to indulge
his soppy dreams
having to ask
the rent is due
the least pretty:
my time for money.

Living statue 1894

I could walk the city for miles
thrilled with its pulse, a streetcar buzz
throbbing in my ears, mansick and drunk
on the veneration of men and their money
stumbling with them into a dazzling round
of dinner, drinks and bed, but it could never
be just money. I was not their equal
despite their private implacable needs
they were cool and distant on the street.

Respectability I left behind like a prison
with no twinge of conscience, hugging bright
independence, went travelling with Henry de Vry
grateful to be employed, earning my way
a sylph in his living tableaux, enacting
classical scenes.

I lived on bread, butter, cigarettes and coffee
saw no one, stayed in bed, read for hours.
Each night stripped naked, whitened all over
transformed to a marble statue of classical proportions:
Psyche, Aphrodite, Ariadne astride my panther.
In the living gallery of magnificent bodies
I loved my metamorphosis, my flawless beauty
anonymous with uncanny power
ritually cleansed, unmoving, unborn.

Else among the camellias

I didn't want their women-worship
I didn't want to be their mother or
have their children—no lemonade-blooded
role for me—I had my dogs, art was to be my expression
I was riding a strong life current.

Wolfi told me I could be a great courtesan
eine Kameliendame, how sickly sweet, the insipid
costume and corsets. Would he have me lose so much
of myself, walk my life asleep, drugged, discreet
so blatantly another's possession and kept
from the kingdom of my mind?

The Kameliendame died alone coughing her
lungs out, loveless, hardly an ad for it, was she?
and only her diary as witness—the likeness
in our stories trivial, the gas in my case hardly as cloying
as her dying flowers, and Pinky-dog there at the end
with me, but how much more pathetic was she
left yearning, lost in the fantasy.

Were we so different, both worn down
in soul and body, a combination of missing teeth, poor
lungs, pallor, swollen feet, and Marie/Marguerite
wracked with consumption, a gift from her partners?
With my vagabond art, guerrilla theatre, I was the athlete
but in hindsight bound to run out of juice. She tied herself
to a regimen of etiquette and illusion—she controlled men
but couldn't control her story; I left a part of me
to tell the tale, chose the place and time
choreographed the final dance.

Palermo: dream sequence

My lover came to say goodbye last night
with his poet's cape and floppy hat
flapping up the stairs, his eyes so sad
going off to his execution by electric chair
for being an imposter and trumped-up spy
my sister sending him off to do his duty
meanwhile stroking me like some pet
one-legged dog. Even so I sensed her
patience waning, but what about them
what were they thinking, with
her bloodless calm, his numb acceptance
their apathy made me crazy! I found
myself in the street naked but for a scarlet
underskirt, embarrassed and trying to hide
my pulchritude. I hurried to the local
hairdresser and that line of women so
familiar: neighbours, mother's friends
all multiplied in the mirror, frozen
in shock, their stares as cold as glass.
I hurried away and further on entered
an ancient coliseum, in its dark interior
squeezing past a row of three iron statues,
all cool metal with erect penises pricking
me as I moved past, finding myself
in a room with a coffin and in it
a woman laid out, her abdomen wriggling
with worms. But I was too anxious
about those statues with their electric
organs blocking my exit to feel
anything for that woman, her body
in a fever of decay.

I've got a new boyfriend

Except he isn't my boyfriend and I'm married but that
doesn't matter, he's such a dazzler. How hopelessly I want
his knees, that waist. My eyes ache from his brilliance,
but I can't stop staring. I am obsessed with his boots,
collar, and suspenders—how they hold him—and realize
I am jealous. I am afraid to touch him with his fashion
hauteur and faultless calm. I memorize his cool lips,
flair for words, the distilled slang spiking his sentences.
A promise of hot blood but humming at a low register.
A glamorous agent with a dark agenda. We sit saying
nothing memorable, all the while I'm burning. I want
to fondle those perfect kneecaps beneath the fabric, cut
narrow and elegant. I'm hopelessly dizzy and yearning,
made clumsy with desire, so naked, fragile, incendiary, I
hate him. Surely he knows this; it is written all over me
in breathless, glowing inks. We are locked in a life-and-
death struggle. I cannot meet those Norse-god eyes, but
I will melt him and claim his reluctant shudder beneath
me.

Frau Endell's letter from the spa to Felix Greve

Felix I miss your society, and console
myself that being treated for hysteria
I feel more alive than all those
suffering neurasthenics we count as friends.

When you come, please bring the key
to my husband's riding breeches.
The breeches are in the trunk August is sending
—the key is for the trunk—perhaps you
can slip into them if they are not
too constraining and we will go riding.

The doctor and his wife may read
my letters. I only hope they find them
symptomatic of a wife whose womb
is so excitable, whose desires are so
unbecoming.

Emperor Tse

In a dream and miracle-waiting state, I thought he'd do,
and wrote "Dear August" though something inside me
knew only a future king can pull off a name like Julian or
Augustus. Yet thinking myself talentless, and yes wishing
to share his laurels, I chose him, said "marry me." Friends
looked on in horror—I wasn't exactly a safe bet—and
Gus was seen as the 'great one' in the Berlin pantheon
of applied art and architecture. Yet so convinced of my
queenliness he agreed, calling me Ti, a consort to his Tse.
We wed in imperial yellow and the world spread out at
our feet.

The wedding gave us permission but came with no
fireworks, in fact the licence only uncovered our
sextroubles. I grew resentful and bitchy, and my husband
spared no expense to make things right, after all the
doctor owed him money. Filled with acid and contempt
I was sent to have my womb massaged while His
Impotence stayed at home confident in his bill of health.
Returning after my treatment was like coming home to
prison, and feeling within my sexrights, I took a lover,
and then wide awake walked out the door.

At first Felix felt sorry for him and Gus came with us
on our travels, a festering grudge, reproachful spook, a
seasick wimpie. Finally Felix lost patience, bought him a
bicycle and sent him off to Ischia to get his life in balance
or break his neck.

To the Prince of Dark Waters

for Felix

Your sleek boats, fleet, crisp, and attentive
dog my movements with the ardour of a suitor

whose leather jacket crackles with excitement.
A submariner in the seas of desire

you pretend to swim in my slipstream
calm strokes, your grace outlined in starry foam

over icy intentions, deep and undetected
you write with squid's ink on the waters.

Steely-eyed, a son of obscure nobility, sprung
fully loaded from the loins of Hermes, iridescent

organs shine beneath your self-reliance; the heart
beating its uncoded signals, an aqueous undersong.

Your torpedo dreams break open my innards
shooting through me silver, rubies, and ultramarine

I am flooded, lost, going down as you rise.
Fishes will nibble my toes dressing me as a bride

in the whiteness of my bones. I will savour
your slow descent, your last stumble into my arms.

A sonnet for Fanny E. 1904

Fine golden specks dot the surface of the pool
a spineless life teems on its stagnant edge.
Blue butterflies float in the purple air
stiff palmettos fan, a fragrance hovers.
The garden is abandoned to the rising moon
busy polishing the patina of the broad-leafed fig
as fiery blooms with saffron centres fade
and pale-hued buds open glowing mouths.
Now the crescent hides in the fig tree's top
like a glowing destiny brought to focus
the tall fronds stiffen in the long dark shadows
a blue-armoured dragonfly halts by the pool.
Sedately the slender moon dances out of the trees
dull ache floats before me on a soundless breeze.

Felix the Great

1

In that circle of male friends
conversation turned
around art and music
with undercurrents
of influence and sex.
What was Felix up to?
A cat among pigeons
beautifully dressed
and saying nothing.
Unlike them
he burned
at a higher wattage
ein Übermensch
teasing meaning
from foreign books
sixty-two translations in two
years, nine months.

2

He lost interest in a game
he couldn't win
got lost in translation
poet, farmer, gentleman, crook.
Took his tactical strengths to
America, a new and primitive world
opening before him, forsaking
all thoughts of Friedrich der Große
a life of culture and privilege
he reinvented himself as
an executive business man
Fred the American potato king.

3

In America he wrote me out of the story.
I found work in a cigarette factory
camped out with the Negro workers
till some white trash knocked out
my side teeth, and where was Fritzi
missing in action, *sans souci* with his
full set of teeth. Felix, you ingrate
you so-much-less-than-great
may you be hounded by guilt for
all your desertions
you and the boat you rowed in on
let them bury you with the dogs.

I am in locomotion: a manifesto 1916

I am in locomotion
with loose and tireless pace
my thrust and parrying hips
in supple, tumbling action
I write better for the air
my body, breath, my work and art.
You cannot fault my courage
and what I have I share
and what I take is given, mostly
discards, what you would junk.
I open my doors to strays and dogs
wear trousers and bathe in public
fountains. I swim and shake
cry out and moan
I write you with my body
saying those words you fear and
sign my name in dragon blood.

I am the rival of any man in art:
watch me wear the cock and tails
red tail lights on my coat
blink as I glide about the city
telling the world I'm here
an empress of the streetlights
a cake and all its candles
a Nileless queen. Oh America
I am the mother of your new age
so says Else von Freedom Lovinghaven.
I'm no statue, yes strong, but limber
I'm no virgin stuck on an island
carrying a torch for greed and lust, but
electric, mobile, I am your *Liberty*.

Berenice Abbott: 3 portraits of Else Shakespeare

In time
everything
is rendered
beautiful
by light.

1
Else Shakespeare did what she wanted
damn the cost, opened all those boxes
spread her legs for the going adventure.
Who here could hear her, know her
as other than misrule, disorder?
She kept house in her own fashion
never constrained by five small rooms
defrosting a fridge or machines that
can't comprehend desire.
Given her nature she could never
stay indoors or between the lines
she was always moving
how could you not marvel—
she never denied who she was.
I can still see her
coming up the street before me—
—she had a wonderful stride.

2

When I returned to America
Pinky, her dog, remembered me,
the Baroness saluted me, as one high priestess
to another, drawing imaginary lines
from hip to hip, head to hymen.
She had me believe
a crazy kid from Ohio
could take on Europe, André Gide et al.
made me believe I didn't need
the old ideas of what sculpture was
I could be myself, anywhere, what
no one expected, with what came to hand
despite the scepticism of mentors
I could sculpt with light and shadow
images luminous with time.

3

She started out alive and buzzing
a crazy Pomeranian kid who
wore a paintbox round her neck
and said: *I give the world its colour*
and then turned herself to marble
padded and whitened for an ancient frieze
and gave her life over to Felix
to sanitize and turn into a book
that ends abruptly with the heroine's death.
The idea a prelude to his play death
the new American business sense
and a deletion of Else from his life.
He left her to take this in her stride
making herself a work of art
with the cast-off bits of city junk and
trinkets, enacting a cubist collage:
a dada caryatid come to life.

~ ~ ~

Her luck to leave such a faint trail
scattered letters, a few artifacts
rare photos,
all but forgotten.
What follows now:
slander, innuendo, lies

     bit by bit
a life
          obscured by legend

          out of focus.

Bride stripped bare: Marcel to queen

...ere I turn to glass and the world around me glassy!
                        — the Baroness

Her graceful torso, back and breasts
the beauty of an ephebe, they said
yet lubricious in eye and mind
stripped bare of restraint, a free
radical, humming with vibration.

I might have been her champion
a witness to her cinematic
blossoming
as pubic queen—
our meetings could never be
determined by
quiet games of chess.

She couldn't fathom I'd win
by stalemate and deferral:
I am not here...
you can leave a message...
I may reply...
comme ci, comme ça...
I am not governed by desire.

Her bachelors were all flunkies
draftsmen, busboys, priests
drawn into her orbit yet fearing
combustion, they kept their distance—
a delay I sought to set in glass—
and so the gendarme checks
his capture, and magnetic queen.

Mars: portrait of Marcel

One day, bright and shiny,
with poplars atwitter
we drove together, Mars and me
purring along, geniuses together
top down, Mars at the wheel, and me
directing, a time capsule speeding into
the future, past known and comfortable
pathways, the commercial routes
leaving behind Paris, Berlin, München.

As the light left us I saw him as a great and
glowing electric bulb emitting
low grade heat, in fact a frozen planet
with so much tidy and locked away
and me a Mars teutonic
a thundering fireball, upsetting
everything, consuming everyone, denying
nothing, yet wretched before him
his pants pressed the way they were, his
elegant fingers, his person groomed and
imponderable, only showing the world
a uniform, his chess face, yet I found
him transparent, and we were no less
a match for each other, him with his
bottled up sex scent, and me a bride
feeding on love gasoline—a combustible
mix together.

I thought I could be patient
the night air coolly washing over us
his scarf flowing out behind him in
elegant feathers, he was an airy bird
with a neck of impossible length
his body exotic and enthralling
his eyes sphinx-like and distant, vainly
I tried to transfix him and his vanity
fed, he flew off, returning to his aerie
atop Manhattan, closing the door, everything
sealed with discretion, leaving me turning over
stalled, breathless in future gear despite
his incandescence, now as then, I'm freezing
small icicles congeal from my tears.

Bill Williams v. the Baroness

I couldn't take my eyes off Dada
I couldn't take my eyes off her
our eyes locked and off we floated
our fiery balloon drawing
Europe and America with us.
It was a setup: those gals in the Village
had my number, had me pegged
as a furtive lover and hesitant sinner.
Come with me, and I will make a man of you.
I drank from her spirit and
yes, said I loved her
sent her a letter and then, reader
turned and ran.

She lived in a filthy tenement
a woman once beautiful
with her clean soul and three dogs
Spam, Mangy and Pant
her collection of recycled junk
the dime store trinkets, purloined umbrellas.
She did merely what I wished to do
her assertions only in acts and works
with legs that walked and talked.
She wasn't caught in our trap
the American dream, she could
see and say more, and said
"let America do better or be damned."

Fixed in her Medusa stare
I kissed her, and then she pursued me
camped out on my street
renaming it Rich from Ridge for what she called
its 'bungalow-bank-account safety.'
One night she had me called from dinner
when I wouldn't come with her, she slugged me.
That did it—I bought a punching bag
and practised—the next time she tried it
I was ready, about 6 o'clock on Park Avenue.
As the city was concluding its business
I flattened her with a stiff right to the mouth
had her arrested, her words to me:
"America is your pitiful arena
you little Napoleon, you coward!"

I was crazy about her
and she was just plain crazy.
She wanted someone to match her courage
someone with nothing to lose.
Her desire to halt my *Hamlet fears*
to oust *the ghost of honeymoon bliss*
not Floss, but what had poisoned
the once-live body of [my] *art.*
I sputtered back:
Physician, heal thyself!

I wanted to help, to lift her from the gutter
did she really think giving me syphilis
would free my mind for serious art?
Am I ashamed I refused her?
The dada rocket went up and crashed
I met my match, a Martian muse
there was nowhere else to take this
our damned, stinking, deflated balloon.

Djuna's song for a repulsive woman

When she was young she slept
with a dog and ran about wild.
In Munich as a dangerous child
she kissed the boys and made them cry
such *gifts she had but didn't keep.*
Her father had to make his kill
and later her womb needed a massage.
She wrote in languages no one knew
affronted all in her trouser suits
smoked up and dragged night into day
broke rules of taste with vulgar poems
made perverse art out of discards and junk.
She'd follow her muse anywhere
into the darkest den, ablaze among those
half awake, asleep to all those who could
do her harm. Her hunger spilled into our
fears and dreams, infected us with her
decadent disease: we rolled with her
beneath dirty sheets, come down these steps
if you dare, young girls lean back everywhere.

When she was old,
she slept with a dog
her trampled soul
made her a saint
and scarified us all.

Where's the husband?

He's focusing his camera   *Endell*
cluttering surfaces
babying his instruments
hiding in his designs
keeping his own counsel
avoiding bicycles
keeping to himself.

He lost interest, marked his place   *the Baron*
sharpened his sabre
traced the transit
of the war's trajectory
exited downstage
chased by a bear
nurtured his dishonour
went off to care for his dead.

He's working, massaging the story   *Felix*
plundering the word hoard
talking up his product
all the while loose change
held in his pockets, jangling
jangling.

jh on the trial: Sumner v. *The Little Review* 1921

The whole tone of the magazine was found wanting—
We make no compromise with the public taste, our motto—
but Joyce alone was named in the brief.
We had more objections to the Baroness from readers
concerning her futurist writing and bold opinions.
Joyce's *Ulysses* had more attention from the P.O.lice, and
I'm not sure which or what they bothered to read.
But we defended them both against a certain fear
of foreign matter, new ideas about women
new ideas, period. Else defended *Ulysses*
in her way, *who wants to hide our joys (Joyce?)*
said Americans in their worship of plumbing
forget their internal workings and are ashamed:

> Joyce like her *merely the bold engineer*
> *of our internal machinery*
> *his "obscenities" never forced or vulgar.*

Better that Else wasn't on the affidavit
Quinn sure she would not help our cause
would lower the whole tone of the proceedings.
Bad enough, Else came to watch with Mina and Mary
—free-minded women made Quinn cranky.
Bad enough, he was defending us
two lesbians, in his mind Margaret at least
well dressed and pretty, and Joyce's writing
though without the "sanction of age and fame"
well worth his services. And where were the
literati with their mighty tongues & pens
hung over, gone to ground, in hiding, ashamed?

We decided to keep mum, object to nothing
even the judge talking down to Margaret, as to a
woman sheltered from the world:
If she had read "Nausicaa" surely
she did not understand its filth?
No surprise we lost, were fined and finger-
printed and had to promise
    WE WOULD BEHAVE
News now that someone in Europe will publish
Ulysses whole, and so we smite our breasts
        —and limp from the field.

Dream of the father

I have been out for hours
wrapped in that old blanket
I find myself face down
in a doorway, my reptile brain
in alarm: I will be taken
for a thief.

I open my eyes
into a splendid room
dark with pockets of incandescence
a richly patterned carpet, an armchair
and the room's main feature
a desk of masterful proportion
and immovable weight.

He has been writing, the ink on the page
still wet and tearing, but not for me
less than a servant, a dirty thief.
His body is laid out and covered
lifeless, or without life parts
yet his hands pull me
and tell me wordlessly
this is home, his benediction
my palms outstretched
my heart open, receiving
a self, newly hatched
and misery my old blanket
flung off, all but forgotten
my velvet dress, once threadbare
now plush and mossy

my hair before bedraggled
now crowned by a brave hat
its ostrich feathers
alive and quivering.

Let the harpy whisper—you are lost, it will end badly
you'll come to your senses—well, I have my senses
I have my hat, my father's hands
I can endure all such tests
I still feel within me
a glittering wealth.

What America meant to me

I wrote English the way I wanted with
a predilection for big guttural sounds
and simple words, packed portmanteau.

Exotic tongues rolled all around me
a great wave of foreign sound
cleansed my ears and crashed on the page.

Why bring my baggage, I had the freedom
of the streets, walked everywhere, met new ideas
trampled all your flabby, puerile patter.

America, with you I shed two husbands,
with you I won a title, in the land of liberty
lifted my skirts above all your objections, forgetting

pecking orders and oppressive protocols,
those Munich art-boys, let alone old
priests of culture with their doors shut.

I didn't dress the part of citizen hausfrau
was no kept woman, the pale reflection
of my American hubbo and his fat wad of cash

never displaying for him bejewelled arms and throat
my satin-flesh, my consuming needs—an alien
—but never complicit in that stranger fiction.

No, in cast-off clothes, cheap glass beads
tea balls, feathers, a shaved pate, the coal
scuttle hat, I married no one, I married my muse.

My eyes were drawn to the flotsam of the streets
I saw junk as sculpture, or a brave new collage
or simply found, anointed objects my ready-made art.

And yes, I sailed back to Europe, my ship foundered
and went down, taking with it my last bit of youth—
all hands on deck—a model throne, my bold designs.

I rode that boat as far as it could take me—
let the others pickle in museums, I was alive
in the world, propelled toward some vivid truth.

I may well be bald: selling papers on the Ku'damm, Berlin 1923

I might well be faceless for all they see
the artists who hurry by my spot
who never buy my newspaper and
rarely look when I pass their table
they see a brown sparrow woman
too tired and ill to utter a warble.
I am embarrassed wanting so much
to be known and not wanting it
in my dire position, still tall
and proud in my feminine soul.

I might as well be bald the more
I retreat inside my skull, whole
hours go by where I pass as a mute
I come and go in awful freedom
and ponder playing my one bright card.
Can I trace a future in the flight
of pigeons? In my condition
they look too plump and edible
for me to focus, a mutual standoff
for I have nothing to offer them.
I become a professional eavesdropper
and entertain myself with tart replies
yet every day faces appear I smile to see
a fine line of the jaw, blue eyes, a bold
profile whom I transform and costume
into exotic beings for me to take
to my too lonely heart, how I long
for a dog of passion, a marvel of a beast
to be my companion on these long days

though I could keep him no better
than he could carry me when
the rough days come and I have
to squawk at bums who would
rob or short me and the cold wind
blows down my neck, while hunger
gnaws at my courage, I fall to
pacing to fight the damp
dictate letters to my solicitors
and so-called friends, begging
for life, holding off the terrifying
shade who eats away my jewelled insides
leaving behind a gaping hollow
a nauseous soul.

At the business end of the leash

She didn't run with a pack
she gave as good as she got
and she was always yapping
some need to be on top
baroness to earth:
       arf arf
       woof woof

She'd take me everywhere
I'd nose and mark while
she'd rummage and look
and see something those others
wandering around in a daze
just didn't get
she had some sense.

But I was more often
at the business end of the leash
reminding her we had to eat
mutt to baroness: give the dog a bone.
And those get-ups, at times
no self-respecting pooch
would want to be her lead
the shaved head and metal hat
those spoon armoured dresses
tinkle
      tinkle crash
          clang!

Living with her could be some trial
she'd lock me in the closet
when the suits and uniforms came.
She'd take in strays, a lousy bunch
who'd fornicate about the place
and then those mice, the bums
would rush in only after
the breadman had left his loaves
and as quickly flee
when the crumbs were gone.

But she'd get down off her hind legs,
nose to nose, and let me lick her.
She shared her food and let me sleep
curled up beside her in her bed.
We talked: I'd cock my head
and pretend to listen; she cooed to me
and didn't show her teeth
I was her favourite—she was
top drawer—wag wag
        wag wag.

The wake

We find no body but this last supper
a woman made of bread
her nakedness the colour of wheat
a flesh loaf, life-sized
laid out on a stark table.
We are invited to cannibalize
her as we had done in life.
Aghast, and even needled by guilt
somehow everyone manages to eat.

Berenice pouting complains about
having to park camera and flash outside.
Pound in a white suit and goatee
remarks "not much meat on her
and what there is, is tough."
Tom Eliot tells Djuna "darling
go ahead, don't worry about her
take only what you need," while Margaret A.
plump as ever, tuts over the silver plate
the missing damask and absent
Limoges and Fred insists he won't partake
"she's overdone it—she's gone too far."
Billy boy laughs "what would you know
you prairie hick," "why you five dollar bill
you medicine man." Bill hits him in the mouth
they roll over and over, the doctor-poet on top

and then the translator, hitting chairs and mourners
while the boppers and bulimiacs, having
drunk all the red wine, Le Sang du Poète
more potent than they believed, laugh too loud
and are falling off chairs. When Marcel arrives
naked, and starts down the stairs spouting
his cool hipster take on art and sex
a food fight breaks out, someone
sets free Else's pet white mice
all hell breaks loose
and the room quickly clears.

Somewhere in the mess
the Baroness enjoys
a quiet puff or two
gathers up the plates
and pauses to stroke
            the ghostly white mice.

NOTES ON THE POEMS

Maybe
The subtitles in this sequence (vielleicht, kann sein, es mag sein, die Möglichkeiten) translate as: perhaps, maybe, it may be, the possibilities.

Extraordinary food for extraordinary dogs
Between 1920 and 1922 Else wrote two "Subjoy Ride" poems composed from advertising slogans.

P-daddy
"Abel Sanders" was a pseudonym that Ezra Pound used when he published in *The Little Review* while he was its foreign editor.

Goldelse
Goldelse is the nickname that Berliners gave the angel Viktoria atop the Siegessäule (victory column) that commemorates Prussian victories over Austria, Denmark, and France. The

victory over France in 1870 precipitated the emergence of Germany as a modern nation state the following year. Goldelse is the heroine of a popular and eponymously entitled 1866 novel by Eugenie Marlitt.

Else among the camellias
Else studied art in Dachau and later went to Munich, where Karl Wolfskehl introduced her to some of the artists and writers who formed an adoring circle around the poet Stefan George. In Munich she first met August Endell.

Emperor Tse
Tse is the name August Endell (1871–1925), Else's first husband, gave himself.

To the Prince of Dark Waters
Felix Paul Greve in his youth was a great swimmer and oarsman. At the rowing club where he was a member, his nick name was Nixe or "mermaid/merman."

A sonnet for Fanny E. 1904
Between 1904 and 1905 Greve and Else collaborated on a series of poems that were published under the joint pseudonym Fanny Essler.

Felix the Great
Friedrich der Große or Friedrich II, 1720–1786, banished his wife Elizabeth Christine from his court after he became king. In fact she never set foot in Sans Souci, the magnificent palace he had built by Schinkel in Potsdam. While he was a great general and military strategist, his court attracted intellectuals and artists. Frederick the Great is buried at Sans Souci with his horse and dogs.

Berenice Abbott
Abbott, who became a famous photographer, began her career as a sculptor. When she first went to Paris she worked as Man Ray's photographic assistant. Abbott brought with her a letter of introduction written by the Baroness to André Gide, who in the end befriended and was helpful to Abbott.

Bill Williams v. the Baroness
Floss was the nickname of William Carlos Williams's wife Florence.

The bride stripped bare
Between 1915 and 1923 Marcel Duchamp created a work on two large glass panels which came to be entitled "The Large Glass" or "The Bride Stripped Bare by Her Bachelors, Even." Duchamp was a chess afficionado.

jh on the trial
Jane Heap, who along with Margaret Anderson edited *The Little Review (LR)*, signed herself in the magazine "jh." John Quinn was a lawyer, art collector, and friend of Ezra Pound, who subsidized the publication of *The Little Review*. The Baroness published a defence of Joyce in the *LR* entitled "The Modest Woman."

BARONESS ELSE VON FREYTAG LORINGHOVEN

The Baroness Else von Freytag Loringhoven was born Else Hildegard Plötz in 1874 in the town of Swinemünde on the Baltic Sea in what is now Poland. She grew up in a relatively prosperous, middle-class family. Her father was a master mason and her mother a cultured woman from a family of impoverished gentility. Else had one sister, Charlotte Louise, a year younger. Her mother died when Else was eighteen, having suffered from mental decline for a number of years before her death, possibly as a result of syphilis contracted from Else's father. Three months after her mother's death Adolph Plötz married a woman whom Else describes as wearing "the bourgeois harness of respectability from morning to night." Finding she could not live in her stepmother's house at eighteen, with no money, no practical experience or training, and no knowledge of the world, Else ran away to Berlin, where she initially lived with a spinster aunt who was a shopkeeper. She never returned to Swinemünde and had little contact with her family after that.

In Berlin Else tried to pursue a career on stage. During this time she appeared in Henry de Vry's theatre of "living marbles," where as a member of his troupe she enacted classical tableaux. After quarrelling with her disapproving aunt, who had initially supported her financially, she found her acting ambitions impeded by poverty. She turned to male admirers for assistance. During this time she was treated for syphilis in a sanatorium and "cured." The medical staff told her that her infection was congenital. The disease appears not to have caused her great suffering or incapacity after that. She even wrote that the disease was an affliction that made her strong and gave her "dragon blood." Else believed in free love, and the stigma of the disease did not inhibit her sexual activity.

Eventually she found friends and kindred spirits in the fin-de-siècle artistic circles in Munich and there she met her first husband, the architect and designer August Endell. Few of his Jugendstil buildings remain; considered decadent by the Nazis, some were demolished in the 1930s. Today he is best known for his work on the design of the Hackesche Höfe in Berlin and for his theoretical writings. She met the writer and translator Felix Paul Greve while married to Endell, and the relationship was initially encouraged by him. About this time Else was sent to a sanatorium for a rest cure allegedly because her sexual desires intimidated Endell. In 1903 Else ran away with Felix and soon learned he was a pathological liar. Later that year he was sent to prison for fraud and after his prison term they lived as if husband and wife in various places in Europe. They married in Berlin in 1907.

Perhaps facing other criminal charges, and giving up his dream of becoming a successful writer in Europe, Greve faked his suicide in 1909 and went to America, where he created a new identity for himself as Frederick Philip Grove (FPG). Else followed him to Sparta, Kentucky, where they lived briefly on a small farm until he abandoned her in 1911. She never saw him again. (He later emerged as a school teacher in Manitoba and a writer of prairie realist novels

Settlers of the Marsh and *Fruits of the Earth*, which were only published after Else had returned to Europe.) Else made her way to New York, where she met the German Baron Leopold von Freytag Loringhoven. They were married in 1913. A year later he went back to Europe to enlist in the German army but was taken prisoner when his ship landed in France. He committed suicide while interned in Switzerland in 1919.

Else became involved in the Dada art scene in New York, at first through her friendship with Marcel Duchamp. She had written poetry with FPG, but it had been in the style of German romantic poetry. Although she had dabbled in art in Germany, in New York she worked more seriously, producing collages, ready-mades, and sculptures. A famous one of Duchamp was composed of "a metallic gear and clock spring intermixed with feathers and twigs in a wine glass overlaid with a cog wheel and feather on top of what looks like a fishing pole and line." Her writing was also experimental; she wrote sound poetry and used 'found poetry' in her Dada poem "Subjoy Ride," her "Ready to Wear, American Soul Poetry." It was in New York City that she developed into the fearless, eccentric, uncompromising character that prompted Jane Heap, one of the editors of *The Little Review*, to call her the "first American Dada." Part of her eccentricity was the manner in which she dressed, so that she could be called an early performance artist or proto-punk. A number of contemporaries wrote about her highly unusual appearance. In one outfit she put together a kilt, a bolero jacket, dime-store bangles on her arms, spoons hanging from her hat, spats on her feet and tea balls hanging from her breasts. On other occasions, she could appear with a shaved head painted vermilion, with stockings painted on her legs, or with a coal scuttle on her head. She had a wide sphere of acquaintance and influence. FPG wrote two novels in German largely inspired by her life. Man Ray and Duchamp made an experimental film with her called "The Baroness Shaving her Pubic Hair." According to the photographer Berenice Abbott "the Baroness was like Jesus Christ and Shakespeare all rolled into one and perhaps she was the most influential person to me in the early part of my life." The character Robin Wood in

Djuna Barnes's novel *Nightwood* is said to be based on Else. "Kassandra Else" appears in Pound's *Cantos*, and it is said that Wallace Stevens would not venture above a certain street in the Village for fear of running into her. She had a brief incendiary relationship with William Carlos Williams, which he documented in various autobiographical writings.

Else was very poor in New York and tried to support herself through her art and as an artist's model. Eventually she tired of American philistinism and prudishness and managed to scrape together enough money from friends to return to Germany in 1923. There she encountered a Germany in postwar depression, suffering from high unemployment and hyper-inflation. In 1926 she was able to get papers to move to Paris to be near friends who could help her. In failing health and selling newspapers to survive, she died in 1927 at the age of fifty-three. She and her dog Pinky were found asphyxiated by gas fumes; she is believed to have taken her own life.

ACKNOWLEDGEMENTS

First and foremost I acknowledge my debt to the Baroness, whose life, art, publications, and papers at the University of Maryland are the basis of this book. No writing would have happened, however, without the intervention of my friend Gaby Divay and her enthusiasm for both Frederick Philip Grove and the Baroness von Freytag Loringhoven. In 1998 Gaby organized a symposium on Grove at the University of Manitoba which included a wonderful panel on the Baroness, and I am grateful to the experts who spoke that day, Gisela Baronin Freytag von Loringhoven (Tübingen, Germany), Irene Gammel (then at the University of Prince Edward Island), and Julia Van Haaften (New York Public Library) for providing the initial inspiration for *Mama Dada*.

I thank the University of Manitoba for allowing me leaves from my work that gave me valuable research and writing time, and in particular I am grateful to my friend and colleague Donna Breyfogle as well as my former director Carolynne Presser for their support. I am grateful as well to the faculty and participants at the Banff Writers Workshop in 2001 who helped nurture this manuscript into existence. I am especially thankful for the writer-in-residency made possible by the University of Western Ontario and the Canada Council for the Arts in 2001/2002 during which this book started to take shape, and for grants from the Manitoba Arts Council that helped it progress.

I thank the following individuals:

George Amabile, Jane Casey, and Barry Dempster, who read earlier versions of my manuscript and gave me valuable feedback and encouragement.

Maureen Scott Harris for her acute reading and insightful suggestions, and for being a shining light in all things.

Dennis Cooley for his literate ear, sense of humour, and uncanny belief in this book.

Douglas Allen for good times, good stories, and literary advice.

Lindy Clubb for her generous friendship and laughter.

Barbara Schott for her clarity, forgiveness, and writing support.

Sean Smith for his keen ear for language and quiet, confident example.

I am particularly indebted to David Darby for his introduction to German and Germany and for his many skills, literary and otherwise, that saw me through this book.

And finally I thank the energetic and supportive team at Turnstone: Todd Besant, Jamis Paulson, and in particular my editor Sharon Caseburg.

Some of the poems in this book were originally published or have been accepted for publication in *CV2*, *Grain*, *Prairie Fire*, and *werd*.

Also by Jan Horner

Elizabeth Went West

Recent Mistakes